M

by Iain Gray

Lang**Syne**

PUBLISHING

WRITING *to* REMEMBER

LangSyne

PUBLISHING

WRITING *to* REMEMBER

79 Main Street, Newtongrange,
Midlothian EH22 4NA
Tel: 0131 344 0414   Fax: 0845 075 6085
E-mail: info@lang-syne.co.uk
www.langsyneshop.co.uk

Design by Dorothy Meikle
Printed by Ricoh Print Scotland
© Lang Syne Publishers Ltd 2013

ISBN 978-1-85217-532-0

Miller

MOTTO:
My hope is in God.

CREST:
A blue wolf's head.

NAME variations include:
Millar
Millers

Chapter one:

The origins of popular surnames

by George Forbes and Iain Gray

If you don't know where you came from, you won't know where you're going is a frequently quoted observation and one that has a particular resonance today when there has been a marked upsurge in interest in genealogy, with increasing numbers of people curious to trace their family roots.

Main sources for genealogical research include census returns and official records of births, marriages and deaths – and the key to unlocking the detail they contain is obviously a family surname, one that has been 'inherited' and passed from generation to generation.

No matter our station in life, we all have a surname – but it was not until about the middle of the fourteenth century that the practice of being identified by a particular surname became commonly established throughout the British Isles.

Previous to this, it was normal for a person to be identified through the use of only a forename.

But as population gradually increased and there were many more people with the same forename, surnames were adopted to distinguish one person, or community, from another.

Many common English surnames are patronymic in origin, meaning they stem from the forename of one's father – with 'Johnson,' for example, indicating 'son of John.'

It was the Normans, in the wake of their eleventh century conquest of Anglo-Saxon England, a pivotal moment in the nation's history, who first brought surnames into usage – although it was a gradual process.

For the Normans, these were names initially based on the title of their estates, local villages and chateaux in France to distinguish and identify these landholdings.

Such grand descriptions also helped enhance the prestige of these warlords and generally glorify their lofty positions high above the humble serfs slaving away below in the pecking order who had only single names, often with Biblical connotations as in Pierre and Jacques.

The only descriptive distinctions among the peasantry concerned their occupations, like 'Pierre the swineherd' or 'Jacques the ferryman.'

Roots of surnames that came into usage in England not only included Norman-French, but also Old French, Old Norse, Old English, Middle English, German, Latin, Greek, Hebrew and the Gaelic languages of the Celts.

The Normans themselves were originally Vikings, or 'Northmen', who raided, colonised and eventually settled down around the French coastline.

The had sailed up the Seine in their longboats in 900AD under their ferocious leader Rollo and ruled the roost in north eastern France before sailing over to conquer England in 1066 under Duke William of Normandy – better known to posterity as William the Conqueror, or King William I of England.

Granted lands in the newly-conquered England, some of their descendants later acquired territories in Wales, Scotland and Ireland – taking not only their own surnames, but also the practice of adopting a surname, with them.

But it was in England where Norman rule and custom first impacted, particularly in relation to the adoption of surnames.

This is reflected in the famous *Domesday Book*, a massive survey of much of England and Wales, ordered by William I, to determine who owned what, what it was worth and therefore how much they were liable to pay in taxes to the voracious Royal Exchequer.

Completed in 1086 and now held in the National Archives in Kew, London, 'Domesday' was an Old English word meaning 'Day of Judgement.'

This was because, in the words of one contemporary chronicler, "its decisions, like those of the Last Judgement, are unalterable."

It had been a requirement of all those English landholders – from the richest to the poorest – that they identify themselves for the purposes of the survey and for future reference by means of a surname.

This is why the *Domesday Book*, although written in Latin as was the practice for several centuries with both civic and ecclesiastical records, is an invaluable source for the early appearance of a wide range of English surnames.

Several of these names were coined in connection with occupations.

These include Baker and Smith, while Cooks, Chamberlains, Constables and Porters were to be found carrying out duties in large medieval households.

The church's influence can be found in names such as Bishop, Friar and Monk while the popular name of Bennett derives from the late fifth to mid-sixth century Saint Benedict, founder of the Benedictine order of monks.

The early medical profession is represented by Barber, while businessmen produced names that include Merchant and Sellers.

Down at the village watermill, the names that cropped up included Millar/Miller, Walker and Fuller, while other self-explanatory trades included Cooper, Tailor, Mason and Wright.

Even the scenery was utilised as in Moor, Hill, Wood and Forrest – while the hunt and the chase supplied names that include Hunter, Falconer, Fowler and Fox.

Colours are also a source of popular surnames, as in Black, Brown, Gray/Grey, Green and White, and would have denoted the colour of the clothing the person habitually wore or, apart from the obvious exception of 'Green', one's hair colouring or even complexion.

The surname Red developed into Reid, while

Blue was rare and no-one wanted to be associated with yellow.

Rather self-important individuals took surnames that include Goodman and Wiseman, while physical attributes crept into surnames such as Small and Little.

Many families proudly boast the heraldic device known as a Coat of Arms, as featured on our front cover.

The central motif of the Coat of Arms would originally have been what was borne on the shield of a warrior to distinguish himself from others on the battlefield.

Not featured on the Coat of Arms, but highlighted on page three, is the family motto and related crest – with the latter frequently different from the central motif.

Adding further variety to the rich cultural heritage that is represented by surnames is the appearance in recent times in lists of the 100 most common names found in England of ones that include Khan, Patel and Singh – names that have proud roots in the vast sub-continent of India.

Echoes of a far distant past can still be found in our surnames and they can be borne with pride in commemoration of our forebears.

Chapter two:

Invasion and conquest

Ranked at 52nd in some lists of the 100 most common surnames in England, 'Miller' was originally an occupational name denoting someone who operated a mill, such as a corn mill.

Of English, Scottish and German roots it derives from the Old Norse 'mylwari', later the Middle English 'mille', indicating a mill.

In common with many other English surnames, it was first popularised in the wake of the Norman Conquest of 1066 – but the ancestors of those who would come to adopt it were present throughout the British Isles from a much earlier date.

This means that flowing through the veins of many bearers of the Miller name today may well be the blood of those Germanic tribes who invaded and settled in the south and east of Britain from about the early fifth century.

Known as the Anglo-Saxons, they were composed of the Jutes, from the area of the Jutland Peninsula in modern Denmark, the Saxons from Lower Saxony, in modern Germany and the Angles from the Angeln area of Germany. It was the Angles who gave the name 'Engla land', or 'Aengla land' – better known as 'England.'

They held sway from approximately 550 to 1066, with the main kingdoms those of Sussex, Wessex, Northumbria, Mercia, Kent, East Anglia and Essex.

Whoever controlled the most powerful of these kingdoms was tacitly recognised as overall 'king' – one of the most noted being Alfred the Great, King of Wessex from 871 to 899.

It was during his reign that the famous *Anglo-Saxon Chronicle* was compiled – an invaluable source of Anglo-Saxon history – while Alfred was designated in early documents as *Rex Anglorum Saxonum*, King of the English Saxons.

Other important Anglo-Saxon works include the epic *Beowulf* and the seventh century *Caedmon's Hymn*.

Through the Anglo-Saxons, the language known as Old English developed, later transforming from the eleventh century into Middle English – sources from which many popular English surnames of today, such as Miller, derive.

The Anglo-Saxons meanwhile, had usurped

the power of the indigenous Britons – who referred to them as 'Saeson' or 'Saxones.'

It is from this that the Scottish Gaelic term for 'English people' of 'Sasannach' derives, the Irish Gaelic 'Sasanach' and the Welsh 'Saeson.'

We learn from the *Anglo-Saxon Chronicle* how the religion of the early Anglo-Saxons was one that pre-dated the establishment of Christianity in the British Isles.

A form of Germanic paganism, with roots in Old Norse religion, it shared much in common with the Druidic 'nature-worshipping' religion of the indigenous Britons.

It was in the closing years of the sixth century that Christianity began to take a hold in Britain, while by approximately 690 it had become the 'established' religion of Anglo-Saxon England.

The first serious shock to Anglo-Saxon control came in 789 in the form of sinister black-sailed Viking ships that appeared over the horizon off the island monastery of Lindisfarne, in the northeast of the country.

The monastery was sacked in an orgy of violence and plunder, setting the scene for what would be many more terrifying raids on the coastline of not only England, but also Wales, Ireland and Scotland.

But the Vikings, or 'Northmen', in common with the Anglo-Saxons of earlier times, were raiders who eventually stayed – establishing, for example, what became Jorvik, or York, and the trading port of Dublin, in Ireland.

Through intermarriage, the bloodlines of the Anglo-Saxons also became infused with that of the Vikings.

But there would be another infusion of the blood of the 'Northmen' in the wake of the Norman Conquest – a key event in English history that sounded the death knell of Anglo-Saxon supremacy.

By 1066, England had become a nation with several powerful competitors to the throne.

In what were extremely complex family, political and military machinations, the English monarch was Harold II, who had succeeded to the throne following the death of Edward the Confessor.

But his right to the throne was contested by two powerful competitors – his brother-in-law King Harold Hardrada of Norway, in alliance with Tostig, Harold II's brother, and Duke William II of Normandy.

In what has become known as The Year of Three Battles, Hardrada invaded England and gained victory over the English king on September 20 at the battle of Fulford, in Yorkshire.

Five days later, however, Harold II decisively defeated his brother-in-law and brother at the battle of Stamford Bridge.

But he had little time to celebrate his victory, having to immediately march south from Yorkshire to encounter a mighty invasion force, led by Duke William of Normandy, that had landed at Hastings, in East Sussex.

Harold's battle-hardened but exhausted force of Anglo-Saxon soldiers confronted the Normans on October 14 in a battle subsequently depicted on the Bayeux tapestry – a 23ft. long strip of embroidered linen thought to have been commissioned eleven years after the event by the Norman Odo of Bayeux.

Harold drew up a strong defensive position at the top of Senlac Hill, building a shield wall to repel Duke William's cavalry and infantry.

The Normans suffered heavy losses, but through a combination of the deadly skill of their archers and the ferocious determination of their cavalry they eventually won the day.

Anglo-Saxon morale had collapsed on the battlefield as word spread through the ranks that Harold had been killed – the Bayeux Tapestry depicting this as having happened when the English king was struck by an arrow to the head.

Amidst the carnage of the battlefield, it was difficult to identify him – the last of the Anglo-Saxon kings.

Some sources assert William ordered his body to be thrown into the sea, while others state it was secretly buried at Waltham Abbey.

What is known with certainty, however, is that William in celebration of his great victory founded Battle Abbey, near the site of the battle, ordering that the altar be sited on the spot where Harold was believed to have fallen.

William was declared King of England on December 25, and the complete subjugation of his Anglo-Saxon subjects followed.

Those Normans who had fought on his behalf were rewarded with the lands of Anglo-Saxons, many of whom sought exile abroad as mercenaries.

Within an astonishingly short space of time, Norman manners, customs and law were imposed on

England – laying the basis for what subsequently became established 'English' custom and practice.

But beneath the surface, old Anglo-Saxon culture was not totally eradicated, with some aspects absorbed into those of the Normans, while faint echoes of the Anglo-Saxon past is still seen today in the form of popular surnames such as Miller.

First recorded in the English county of Sussex in 1327, it is a name that features prominently in the historical record.

Chapter three:

Honours and distinction

An impressive number of bearers of the proud name of Miller have stamped their mark on the historical record of the sciences, while others have gained distinction on the bloody field of battle.

Born in 1691, Phillip Miller was the eminent Scottish botanist who wrote influential works that include his 1724 *The Gardener's and Florists Dictionary or a Complete System of Horticulture* and the 1731 *The Gardener's Dictionary containing the Methods of Cultivating and Improving the Kitchen Fruit and Flower Garden.*

Little is known of his early life, but it is known that from 1722 until shortly before his death in 1771 he served as the chief gardener at what was then the Chelsea Physic Garden.

Corresponding with other botanists and obtaining a wide range of plants from throughout the world and introducing them to Britain for the first time, it was said of him by his contemporaries that he raised the reputation of the Chelsea Garden so much that it excels all the gardens of Europe for its amazing variety of plants of all orders and classes from all climates."

Said to have possessed a knowledge of plants that was unsurpassed in his lifetime, he was honoured by election as a Fellow of the prestigious scientific 'think-tank', The Royal Society.

Another member of the Royal Society was the Welsh mineralogist and crystallographer William Hallowes Miller, born in 1801 near Llandovery, Carmarthenshire.

Graduating from St John's College, Cambridge he worked for a time as one of its tutors and published studies on both hydrodynamics and hydrostatics, while in 1832 he was promoted to the post of professor of mineralogy at the college.

The author of important works that include his 1839 *Crystallography*, he died in 1880, while the mineral known as *millerite* is named in his honour.

Not only a self-taught geologist but also a writer, folklorist and evangelical Christian, Hugh Millar was born in Cromarty, in the north east of Scotland, in 1802.

Apprenticed as a stonemason when he was aged 17, his interest in geology was fired by examining rocks in the quarries in which he worked and by exploring the rugged Cromarty coastline.

Publishing a volume of poems in 1829 and, five years later, his *Scenes and Legends in the North of Scotland* from 1840 he worked as the editor of the evangelical Christian newspaper the *Witness*.

But it is for his geological work that he is best known today, publishing major works that include his 1841 *The Old Red Sandstone*, the 1850 *Footprints of the Creator* and, in the year of his death in 1856, *The Testimony of the Rocks*.

Miller was of the firm belief that the Earth was of great age and that it had been inhabited by a number of species which had come into being and gone extinct – all evidence, he held, of the direct action of a Creator.

His home in Cromarty is now a geological museum open to the public, while there is a bust of him in the Hall of Heroes at the Wallace Monument in Stirling; the Miller oil field in the North Sea is also named in his honour.

Another inquiring scientific mind was the American electrical engineer John Milton Miller, recognised for his pioneering work on the quartz crystal oscillators, now known as *Miller Oscillators*, and for identifying what is recognised as the *Miller Effect*.

Born in 1882 in Hanover, Pennsylvania and obtaining a doctorate in physics from Yale, he worked as a radio engineer at the United States Navy's Research Laboratory (NRL), serving there throughout the Second World War.

At the end of the conflict, he was awarded America's Distinguished Civilian Service Award for "initiation of the development of a new flexible radio-frequency cable urgently needed in radio and radar equipment which solved a desperate material shortage in the United States during World War II."

Also the recipient in 1953 of the IRE (Institute of Radio Engineers) Medal of Honor for his contributions to the basic knowledge of electron tube theory, radio instruments and measurements, and crystal controlled oscillators, he died in 1962.

Noted for his studies on the origins of life that demonstrated that organic compounds can be created by chemical processes from inorganic substances, Stanley Lloyd Miller was the American chemist and biologist born in 1930 in Oakland, California.

Earning a doctorate in chemistry from the

University of Chicago in 1954, he was professor of chemistry at the University of California, San Diego from 1968; the recipient of a number of honours and awards that included membership of America's National Academy of Science, he died in 2007.

One particularly inventive bearer of the Miller name was the American businessman and inventor Lewis Miller.

Born in Greentown, Ohio in 1829, it was in the latter years of the nineteenth century that he invented the first harvester-reaper machine – the combine harvester – with the blade mounted in front of the driver, to the side of the horse, as opposed to being pulled behind it.

Making a fortune from his invention, he devoted himself to a number of philanthropic projects before his death in 1899 – while his daughter, Mina, married the great inventor Thomas Alva Edison, who was also from Ohio.

From the sciences to architecture, James Miller was the Scottish architect noted for many buildings in Glasgow that include the former Union Bank building in the city's St Vincent Street, his 1901 work on Glasgow Royal Infirmary, his 1901 to 1905 extensions to Glasgow Central railway station and also a number of other railway stations that include the Wemyss Bay station on the Firth of Clyde.

Born in 1860 in Auchtergaven, Perthshire and having started his career as an architect with the Caledonia Railways' drawing office in Glasgow, he died in 1947.

In May of 2013, meanwhile, it was announced that an army of window cleaners was set to embark on an ambitious project to clean all 48,000 separate panes of glass that adorn the roof of Central Station in order to 'brighten it up' for visitors to the 2014 Commonwealth Games.

Bearers of the Miller name have also gained distinction on the field of battle.

Born in 1820, James Miller was a Scottish recipient of the Victoria Cross (VC), the highest award for valour in the face of enemy action for British and Commonwealth forces.

It was while attached to the Bengal Ordnance Depot, Bengal Army, during the Indian Mutiny of 1857 to 1858 that he performed the actions for which he was awarded the honour.

In October of 1857, near Agra, at great personal risk to himself, he braved enemy fire to assist and carry a badly-wounded officer back to an aid station; later achieving the rank of lieutenant and appointed an honorary major in 1882, he died ten years later.

In the carnage of the First World War, James Miller, born in 1890 in Lancashire was an English posthumous recipient of the VC.

He had been a private in the 7th Battalion, The King's Own (Royal Lancaster) Regiment when in July of 1916 at Bazentin-le-Petit, France he was ordered to deliver a vital message, under heavy enemy shell and machine-gun fire, and to bring back a reply 'at all costs.'

Despite being badly wounded after delivering the message, he was able to stagger back and give the much-needed reply before succumbing to his injuries; his VC is now on display at The King's Own Royal (Lancaster Regiment Museum), Lancaster.

Chapter four:

On the world stage

**Born in New York City in 1981 but moving with
her family to London when she was aged just
under a year old, Sienna Miller is the actress,
model and fashion designer whose film credits
include the 2001 *Kensington*, the 2005 *Casanova*
and the 2012 *Just Like a Woman*.**

Television credits include the 2002 *Bedtime*
and the 2012 *The Girl*, for which she was nominated
for a Golden Globe Award for Best Actress, Mini-
Series or Television Film, and a BAFTA TV Award
for Best Actress.

The recipient of a star on the Hollywood
Walk of Fame, Johnnie Collier was the American
singer, dancer and actress better known by her stage
name of **Ann Miller**.

Best remembered for her work in a number
of Hollywood musicals that include the 1948 *Easter
Parade*, the 1949 *On the Town* and the 1953 *Kiss Me
Kate*, she was also famed for her speed in tap
dancing.

Another of her claims to fame is that she is

recognised as having popularised in the 1940s the wearing of ladies' pantyhose, or tights.

This was after experiencing the problem of repeatedly tearing her stockings during the filming of dance numbers and, at her request, hosiery was manufactured for her as a single pantyhose.

With other major film credits that include the 1940 *Too Many Girls*, the 1941 *Go West, Young Lady*, the 1951 *Texas Carnival* and the 2001 *Mulholland Drive*, she died in 2004.

Born in 1972 in Kingston upon Thames, Jonathan Lee Miller is the English actor of television and film better known as **Jonny Lee**.

The maternal grandson of the late actor Bernard Lee, famous for his role of 'M' in the first eleven James Bond films, his big screen credits include the 1995 *Hackers*, the 1996 *Trainspotting*, the 2006 *The Flying Scotsman* – where he played the role of Scots cycling champion Graeme Obree – and, from 2012, *Byzantium*.

In addition to his work in the theatre, his many television credits include *Casualty*, *Emma* and, from 2012, the role of Sherlock Holmes in the American crime drama *Elementary*, while he was married from 1996 to 1999 to the actress Angelina Jolie.

Not only a noted child actor but also known for recording the 1956 popular children's song *Nellie the Elephant*, Carmen Isabella Miller is better known by her stage name of **Mandy Miller**.

Born in 1944 in Weston-Super-Mare, Somerset she was aged seven when she starred beside Alec Guinness in *The Man in the White Suit*, while other screen credits include the 1952 *Mandy*, the 1954 *Dance, Little Lady*, the 1955 *Raising a Riot* and, from 1956, *The Feminine Touch*.

On British television screens, **Steven Miller**, born in 1982 in Stirling, is the Scottish actor best known for his role of Lenny Lyons in the medical drama *Casualty*, while other credits include the *Casualty* spin-off *Holby City* and *The Bill*.

Born in 1919, **Herman Miller** was the American film and television writer and producer whose big screen credits before his death in 1999 included the 1968 film *Coogan's Bluff*, starring Clint Eastwood and, on television, *Man from Atlantis*, *The Virginian* and *Rawhide*.

Not only an actor but also a playwright, **Jason Miller** was born in 1939 in Queens, New York.

The recipient of the 1973 Pulitzer Prize for Drama for his play *That Championship Season*, his big screen credits before his death in 2001 included the 1973 *The Exorcist* – for which he was nominated for an Academy Award for Best Supporting Actor for his role of Father Damien Karras.

Not only a medical doctor but also an opera and theatre director, actor, television presenter, humourist and author, **Dr Jonathan Miller** was born in London in 1934.

First coming to prominence in the early 1960s with Peter Cook, Dudley Moore and Alan Bennett in the satirical production *Beyond the Fringe*, the Cambridge University graduate has served as an associate director of the Royal National Theatre and was also in charge for a time of the Old Vic Theatre.

His books include the 1971 *Censorship and the Limits of Personal Freedom*, the 1983 *The Human Body* and the 1999 *Nowhere in Particular*, while he was knighted in 2002 for his services to music and the arts.

Also in the arts, **Arthur Miller**, born in 1915 in Harlem, New York City is recognised as having been one of the twentieth century's greatest playwrights and essayists.

The second of three children to Polish-Jewish immigrants to the United States, he began his career as a journalist with the student newspaper the *Michigan Daily*, while he penned his first play, *No Villain*, in 1936.

His further great literary output includes his 1940 *The Man Who Had all the Luck*, the 1949 *Death of a Salesman*, the 1953 *The Crucible* and the 1980 *The American Clock*.

Married from 1956 until 1961 to the Hollywood icon Marilyn Monroe and the recipient of a number of honours and awards that include a Pulitzer Prize for Drama, he died in 2005.

Another great literary figure was **Henry Miller**, born in 1891 in Manhattan, New York City.

Specialising in the genre known as surrealism, he wrote a number of acclaimed novels before his death in 1980 that include his 1934 *Tropic of Cancer*, the 1939 *Tropic of Capricorn* and the 1949-1959 trilogy *The Rosy Crucifixion*.

Bearers of the Miller name have also excelled in the highly competitive world of sport – not least on the fields of European football.

Born in Glasgow in 1955, **Willie Miller** is the Scottish former central defender who, between 1972 and 1990, made 558 appearances for Aberdeen – while in 2003, in a poll to mark the club's centenary, he was voted its greatest player of all time. Earning 65 caps playing for Scotland between 1975 and 1989, he managed his former club Aberdeen from 1992 to 1995, while he became an inaugural inductee to the Scottish Football Hall of Fame in 2004.

Born in Glasgow in 1976, **Charlie Miller** is the attacking midfielder who, in addition to playing for teams that include Rangers, Watford, Dundee United, Australian team Brisbane Roar and Clyde, earned a cap playing for Scotland in 2001.

Another Scottish internationalist is **Kenny Miller**, the striker born in Edinburgh in 1979 who has played for teams that include Hibernian, Rangers, Celtic, Derby County and, from 2012, Canadian club Vancouver Whitecaps.

Also on the football pitch, **Liam Miller**, born in Cork in 1981, is the midfielder who, in addition to playing for the Republic of Ireland, has played for clubs that include Celtic, Manchester United and Hibernian.

From sport to music, Alton Glenn Miller was the famed American big band leader, arranger and composer better known as **Glenn Miller**.

Born into a farming family in 1904 in Clarinda, Iowa it was through earning money from milking cows that he was able to buy his first trombone.

After playing in a number of bands and becoming a popular performer on radio with his unique brand of swing music and featuring in a number of films with his Glenn Miller Band that include the 1941 *Sun Valley Serenade* and the 1942 *Orchestra Wives*, he enlisted in U.S. military service during the Second World War.

With what became known as his Army Air Force Band, he performed in morale-boosting tours throughout not only the United States but also in war-torn Britain.

Memorable compositions such as *Moonlight Serenade*, *Pennsylvania 6-5000*, *Chattanooga Choo Choo*, *In the Mood*, *Tuxedo Junction* and *American Patrol* became iconic 'anthems' during the war and remain popular to this day.

Tragedy struck on December 15, 1944 when, flying from RAF Twinwood Farm in Clapham, near Bedford for an engagement in liberated Paris, his aircraft disappeared over the English Channel.

No trace of the aircraft or its passengers and crew has ever been found, while one of the many theories surrounding its fate is that it may have been struck by incendiary bombs jettisoned from RAF bombers returning from a raid over Germany.

The band leader was posthumously inducted into the Grammy Hall of Fame, while a special Grammy Award was established in his memory in 1973 to honour recordings that are at least 25 years old and have qualitative historical value.

Born in Bridgeton, Glasgow in 1949, **Frankie Miller** is the Scottish rock singer and songwriter known for hits that include his 1977 *Be Good to Yourself*, the 1978 *Darlin'*, the 1979 *When I'm Away from You* and fellow Scotsman Dougie McLean's composition *Caledonia*.

He has also written for a number of other artistes and bands who include Johnny Cash, Rod Stewart, Kim Carnes and The Eagles.

The 1999 BBC television documentary *Stubborn Kinda Fella* featured his recovery from a brain haemorrhage he suffered in New York in 1994 while writing material for a band he had formed with Joe Walsh of The Eagles; as an actor, he starred in the 1979 film by Peter McDougall *Just a Boy's Game*.

Born in 1943 in Milwaukee, **Steve Miller** is the American guitarist and songwriter who, along with his Steve Miller Band, formed in 1967, has enjoyed hit albums that include the 1968 *Children of the Future*, the 1973 *The Joker*, the 1977 *Book of Dreams* and, from 1982, *Abracadabra*.

In a much different musical genre, **David Miller** is the American tenor known as a member of the operatic-pop musical group Il Divo.

Born in San Diego in 1973, he has enjoyed hot albums with the band that include their 2004 debut *Il Divo*.

One bearer of the proud name of Miller with a particularly endearing claim to fame is the Scottish poet **William Miller** – fondly known for the children's nursery rhyme *Wee Willie Winkie*.

Born in the Dennistoun area of Glasgow in 1810, ill-health forced him to abandon his medical studies and instead become a carpenter and cabinet-maker.

Known as "The Laureate of the Nursery", it was in 1842 that his *Whistle-binkie: Stories for the Fireside* – containing his famous *Wee Willie Winkie* – was published.

Dogged throughout his lifetime with ill-health, he died in 1872, while a memorial was later erected to him in the Glasgow Necropolis.